se cubes to subtract.   Match each boat to an island.

Write a subtraction story on this boat.

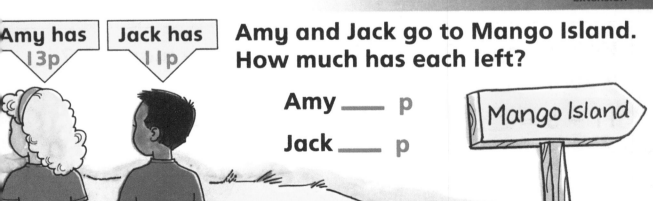

Amy has 13p

Jack has 11p

Amy and Jack go to Mango Island.
How much has each left?

Amy ___ p

Jack ___ p

Mango Island

To land on the island, find numbers which add to 11.

Mango Island

Use counters.

10 + 1				

How many ? ____
3 fly away.

11 − 3 = ____

How many ? ____
7 fall off.

11 − 7 = ____

How many ? ____
5 are picked.

11 − 5 = ____

How many ? ____
9 hide.

11 − 9 = ____

Bushes

Each bush has 11 flowers.   Write stories.

$$9 + 2 = 11$$
$$2 + 9 = 11$$
$$11 - 2 = 9$$
$$11 - 9 = 2$$

$$8 + 3 =$$
$$3 + 8 =$$
$$11 - 3 =$$
$$11 - 8 =$$

$$7 + 4 =$$
$$4 + 7 =$$
$$11 - 4 =$$
$$11 - 7 =$$

$$6 + 5 =$$
$$5 + 6 =$$
$$11 - 5 =$$
$$11 - 6 =$$

Investigation

Find sets of 3 numbers which add to 11.

$$5 + 3 + 3$$

In the jungle

$$\begin{array}{r} 4 \\ +7 \\ \hline \end{array}$$

$$\begin{array}{r} 11 \\ -3 \\ \hline \end{array}$$

$$\begin{array}{r} 3 \\ +8 \\ \hline \end{array}$$

$$\begin{array}{r} 11 \\ -9 \\ \hline \end{array}$$

$$\begin{array}{r} 11 \\ -6 \\ \hline \end{array}$$

$11 - 4 = \underline{\qquad}$

$11 - 8 = \underline{\qquad}$

$5 + 6 = \underline{\qquad}$

$11 - 2 = \underline{\qquad}$

$11 - 1 = \underline{\qquad}$

The nest has 11 eggs.
4 fall out.

How many left? _____

11 flies
5 ants
How many
more flies? _____

$3 + 4 + 4 = \underline{\qquad}$

$5 + 2 + 3 = \underline{\qquad}$

Food

Buying food

5p   6p   4p

3p   CHOCO   CRISPS   2p

How much does each spend?

☐ p   ☐ p   ☐ p

Each child has 11p. They buy these things. How much has each left?

— p   — p   — p

Spend 11p.
What **3** things will you buy?

Nim-Nam-Noo

R 21

Nim-Nam-Noo

Put 12 Nim-nams on the island like this.

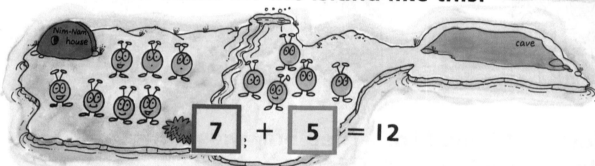

$$\boxed{7} + \boxed{5} = 12$$

Find other ways to put 12 Nim-nams on the island.

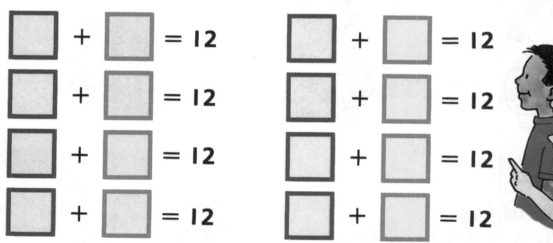

$$\boxed{} + \boxed{} = 12 \qquad \boxed{} + \boxed{} = 12$$

$$\boxed{} + \boxed{} = 12 \qquad \boxed{} + \boxed{} = 12$$

$$\boxed{} + \boxed{} = 12 \qquad \boxed{} + \boxed{} = 12$$

$$\boxed{} + \boxed{} = 12 \qquad \boxed{} + \boxed{} = 12$$

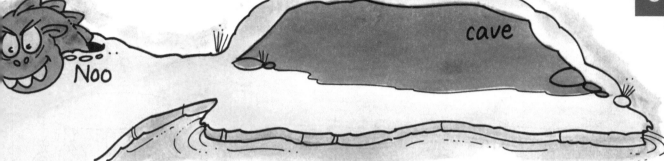

Put 12 Nim-nams on the island like this.

$$\boxed{5} + \boxed{4} + \boxed{3} = 12$$

Find other ways.

$$\boxed{} + \boxed{} + \boxed{} = 12$$

$$\boxed{} + \boxed{} + \boxed{} = 12$$

$$\boxed{} + \boxed{} + \boxed{} = 12$$

Put 12 Nim-nams on the island.

If Noo eats 5, how many are left?

$$12 - 5 = \boxed{}$$

$12 - 9 = \boxed{}$ $12 - 4 = \boxed{}$ $12 - 10 = \boxed{}$

$12 - 7 = \boxed{}$ $12 - 6 = \boxed{}$ $12 - 3 = \boxed{}$

R22

Nim-nams

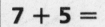

$$7 + 5 =$$

$$12 - 5 =$$
$$12 - 7 =$$

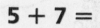

$$5 + 7 =$$

$$9 + 3 =$$
$$3 + 9 =$$
$$12 - 3 =$$
$$12 - 9 =$$

$$6 + 6 =$$
$$12 - 6 =$$

$$8 + 4 =$$
$$4 + 8 =$$
$$12 - 4 =$$
$$12 - 8 =$$

Nim-nam house

ind the answers. Colour them.

red | 7 + 3 | 12 − 10 | 12 − 7
blue | 12 − 4 | 8 + 3 | 6 + 6
green | 6 + 3 | 12 − 9 | 12 − 8

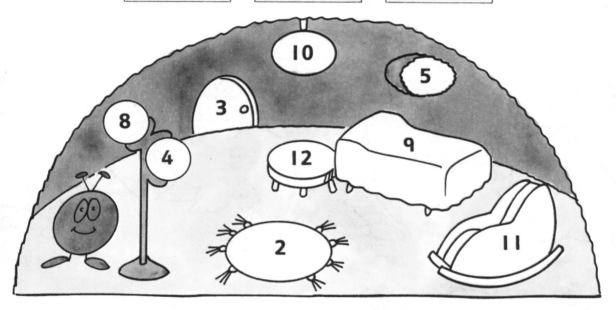

How many altogether?

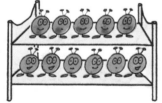

$$\begin{array}{r} 5 \\ +6 \\ \hline \end{array} \qquad \begin{array}{r} 8 \\ +4 \\ \hline \end{array} \qquad \begin{array}{r} 7 \\ +5 \\ \hline \end{array} \qquad \begin{array}{r} 3 \\ +9 \\ \hline \end{array}$$

$$\begin{array}{r} 5 \\ +7 \\ \hline \end{array} \qquad \begin{array}{r} 6 \\ +6 \\ \hline \end{array} \qquad \begin{array}{r} 3 \\ 4 \\ +5 \\ \hline \end{array} \qquad \begin{array}{r} 6 \\ 4 \\ +2 \\ \hline \end{array} \qquad \begin{array}{r} 4 \\ 4 \\ +3 \\ \hline \end{array}$$

To Bear Island

11

Bear Island

In each cave,
colour three bears that add to make 12.

The school cave has

| an even answer greater than 10. |

Write School above the school cave.

11 − 5 =

2
3
+7
___
___

The number before 16 is

Use these numbers to make the sums.

 9 8   4   3

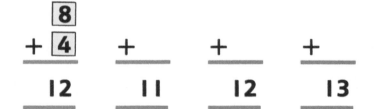

$$
\begin{array}{r} 8 \\ + 4 \\ \hline 12 \end{array}
\qquad
\begin{array}{r} \\ + \\ \hline 11 \end{array}
\qquad
\begin{array}{r} \\ + \\ \hline 12 \end{array}
\qquad
\begin{array}{r} \\ + \\ \hline 13 \end{array}
$$

$$
\begin{array}{r} \\ - \\ \hline 4 \end{array}
\qquad
\begin{array}{r} \\ - \\ \hline 6 \end{array}
\qquad
\begin{array}{r} \\ - \\ \hline 1 \end{array}
\qquad
\begin{array}{r} \\ - \\ \hline 5 \end{array}
$$

To Fun Island

Use 13 counters.

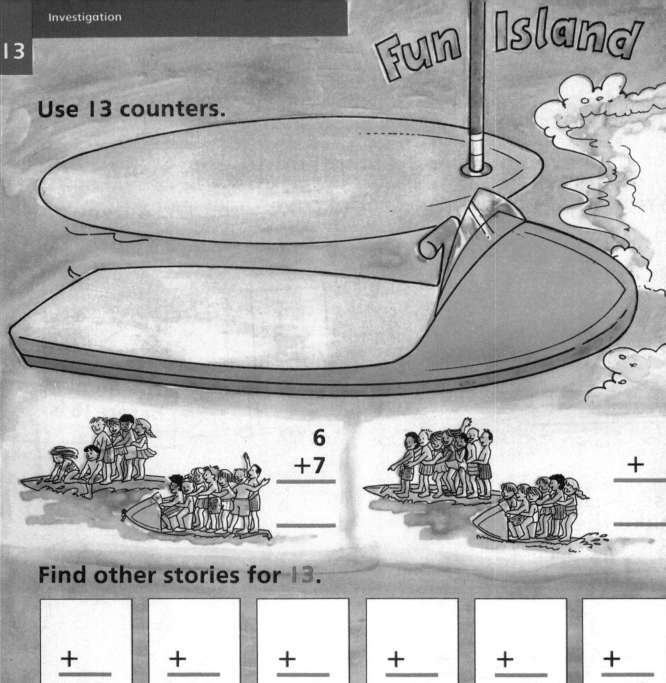

$$6$$
$$+7$$

$$+$$

Find other stories for 13.

+	+	+	+	+	+
13	13	13	13	13	13

$$2 + 3 + 8 = 13$$

Find more stories like this for 13.

$$6 + 7 = 13$$
$$7 + 6 =$$
$$13 - 6 =$$
$$13 - 7 =$$

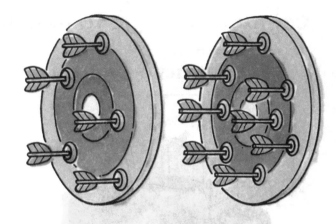

$$5 + 8 =$$
$$8 + 5 =$$
$$13 - 5 =$$
$$13 - 8 =$$

$$9 + 4 =$$
$$4 + 9 =$$
$$13 - 9 =$$
$$13 - 4 =$$

$$10 + 3 \ \ =$$
$$3 + 10 =$$
$$13 - 10 =$$
$$13 - 3 \ \ =$$

R 24

To the train

15

Train ride

Colour a carriage to match each answer.

Spooky Castle

Write the missing number.

| 7 | 9 | 11 | |

This key opens the door. ↑

Cross out
flies to make 13.

13 children go in.
8 come out.

How many
are still in? ____

Add to find the one that is different.

| 6 | 6 | 8 |
| 5 | 7 | 5 |

The trapdoor
key is in it.

Escape

Write the answers.

7 + 6 =

4 + 8 =

12 − 3 =

13 − 4 =

11 − 9 =

7 + 4 =

11 − 4 =

12 − 6 =

13 − 6 =

Colour the boxes

blue if the answer is odd,

red if the answer is even.

| 5 +8 | 12 −9 | 9 +4 | 8 +5 | 7 +5 | 13 −8 |

Which door has an even answer? Colour it red.

Colour three numbers which add to 12.

2

5

3

4

6

Way O

Amy had 13p.
She lost 7p in the sea.

How much is left? —— p

Colour the monster that has two more
black spots than green spots.

To the treasure

Find chests with the same answer.
Colour them to match.

8 + 5

11 − 6

9 + 3

3 + 3 + 7

4 + 7

13 − 8

12 − 1

The treasure is in
the white chest.
Mark it ✗.

R 26

Stickers

Panda 13p

Fox 4p

Badger 6p

Bear 7p

Tiger 5p

Dog 4p

Find the cost of a fox and a bear. ____

Find the cost of a fox, a tiger and a dog . ____

I spend 13p.
I buy 2 animals.
What do I buy? _____

I have 8p.
I want a panda.
How much more do I need? ____

I have 12p. I buy a bear.
What else can I now buy?

fox or _____ or _____

R 27

Prizes

 $+\ 7\ =$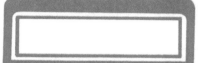

 $-\ 6\ =$

 **Now do these.**

$7 + 9 =$ ☐ $6 + 8 =$ ☐ $10 + 9 =$ ☐

$16 - 7 =$ ☐ $14 - 8 =$ ☐ $17 - 9 =$ ☐

19 **wins a prize**

Who wins a prize? (✓)

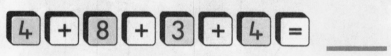

$4 + 8 + 3 + 4 =$ ___

$9 + 2 + 5 + 2 =$ ___

$8 + 6 + 7 - 2 =$ ___

Halves

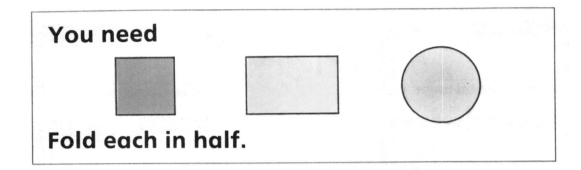

You need

Fold each in half.

Colour one half of each shape.

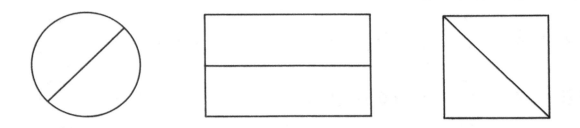

Tick the shapes that show halves.

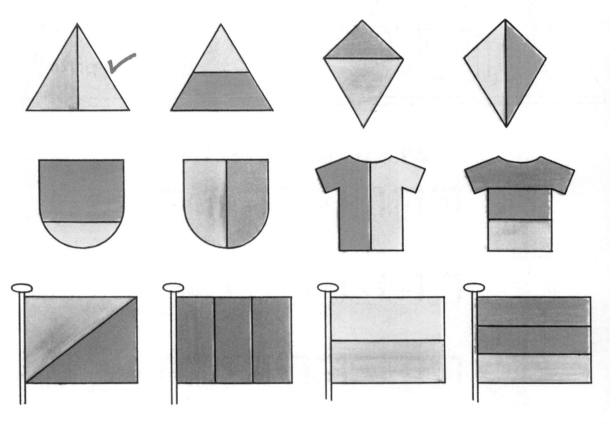

Making halves

Cut out the four-strip.

Fold it in half.

One half of 4 is ＿＿ .

Cut out the six-strip.

Fold it in half.

One half of 6 is ＿＿ .

Make a tower with 8 cubes.

Halve it like this ⟶

One half of 8 is ＿＿ .

Use 10 cubes.

One half of 10 is ＿＿ .

Use cubes.   One half of 12 is ＿＿ .

One half of 16 is ＿＿ .

One half of 20 is ＿＿ .

Quarters

You need

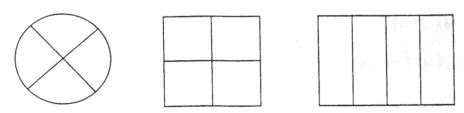

Fold each in quarters.

Colour one quarter of each shape.

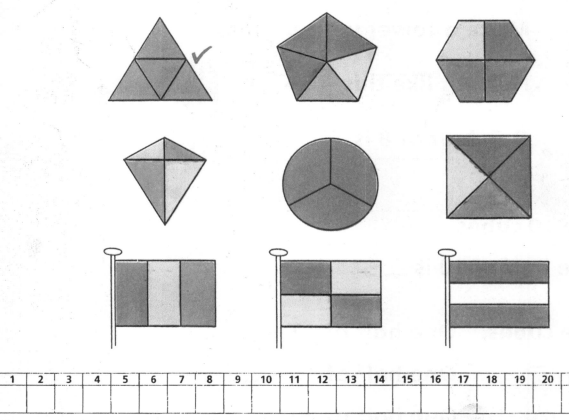

Tick the shapes that show quarters.

1	2	3	4	5	6	7	8	9	10	11	12	13	14	15	16	17	18	19	20	21	22

Heinemann is an imprint of Pearson Education Limited, a company incorporated in England and Wales, having its registered office at Edinburgh Gate, Harlow, Essex, CM20 2JE. Registered company number: 872828
ISBN 978 0 435 03094 0 © Scottish Primary Mathematics Group 1981.
First published 1991. Revised edition 1995.   25   33
Typeset and Illustrated by Oxprint Design. Printed in Great Britain by Bell & Bain Ltd, Glasgow

ISBN 978-0-435030-94-0
9 780435 030940